The Offical Guide to Bad Parenting

by

VERONICAH LARKIN &
CHARLES FIRTH

CHASER BOOKS
Ultimo, Australia

We would like to dedicate this book to our despairing, disappointed, long-suffering, anguished, and eternally heart-broken mothers. Oh, yeah, and fathers too.

We are so fucking sorry.

This edition first published in 2023 by Chaser Books
Building 5B, Level 4, 1 Quay St, Haymarket

The Official Guide to Bad Parenting: 2nd Edition
ISBN 9781760642389

chaser.com.au

Text designed by Charles Firth

Typeset in 13/18 pt Jensen Pro Regular by Charles Firth

Printed and bound by Spotpress, Marrickville.

Introduction
(It's Time to Massively Lower Your Expectations)

There's nothing you need more when you first become a parent than having other parents tell you how you can do it better. Whether it's your slightly-better-looking-than-you high school friend who gives you tips on how to lose your baby bump, or the working mum in your mother's group who nonetheless somehow manages to keep screens away from her kids while running a large construction company, advice about how someone else does things better than you is always welcome.

This is the starting point for this book.

If you're like most people, becoming a parent is the point where you very quickly realise that the only way to survive is to abandon all hope of having the perfect life. While everyone else around you seems to be thriving, for you, getting through a day becomes a major achievement. Of course, you can't admit this to anyone, especially not yourself. Instead, it is important to join the slipstream of Instagram posts sharing the rare moments of joy that come with parenthood.

But with the general despair that accompanies parenthood, also comes an openness to accept advice from places that you would never, ever have gone to before you became a parent. Suddenly, whatever parenting blog gets the top hit on Google becomes the definitive source for questions ranging from the nutrition of your infant, pharmacological dosaging, through to complex gynacological issues.

Of course, here at *The Chaser,* reliability has never been front and centre of anything we do. Which is why we saw an opportunity to create a parenting book with dubious-enough advice that it will eventually rise to the top of the Google-rankings.

We're pretty sure we can profit from your anxiety so we've put together this guide.

But if there's one message you take from the book it should be this: everyone is a 'bad parent'. Your children will eventually blame you for something, it's just a matter of which thing they blame you for.

Parenting can be hard, so you might as well enjoy it along the way. And the best way to do that is to accept that you're a bad parent, just like everyone else. The sooner you realise that, the easier everything will be.

Veronicah Larkin
& Charles Firth
August 2023

GETTING PREGNANT

(OR TURNING SEX INTO SOMETHING DULL AND LIFELESS)

Unfortunately, how people get pregnant is not yet known. For years, experts thought that pregnancy was linked to sex, but the correlation is all over the shop, and some scientists now believe pregnancy is more closely correlated to drinking too much alcohol a few weeks ago.

What does seem to be immutably true is that if you're a couple who is actively trying to get pregnant, it is important that sex becomes as dull and routine

as possible. So here is a modern guide to turning the fiery passion of baby-making into something as thrilling as a tax seminar.

Step 1: Schedule, Schedule, Schedule

Replace spontaneous, passionate rendezvous with a Google calendar invite-based method of sex. Download a 'Pregnancy Planner' app and input your menstrual cycle data, body temperature, and the parliamentary sitting dates. The app will then suggest a series of optimal dates for you to joylessly 'do the deed'. Remember, nothing says romance like a quickie at 3:17pm next Tuesday! Lawyers should link the app to their work calendar. That way, you can bill your partner in 6-minute increments for the time you've taken to screw them, just like you would with a client.

Step 2: Dress For The Occasion

Prepare for parenthood by trading in your lacy lingerie and silk boxers for sensible alternatives. Picture this:

matching flannel pyjamas, woollen socks, and oversized, worn-in T-shirts proudly boasting slogans like 'Property of the Baby Factory' or imprinted with a handy chart of your ovulation cycle.

Step 3: Create A Baby-Making Soundtrack

If you're having to have a lot of sex, replace your sexy mood music playlists with podcasts and audiobooks you need to catch up on. You'll have to learn to multitask as parents anyway, so why not learn that skill along the way!

Step 4: Get Into the Mood First

If you've got half an hour to kill before your scheduled intimacy, use the time to watch something that will get you into the mood. That's right, we're talking about documentaries on parenting techniques from around the world. Be sure to memorise obscure methods involving beta carotene diets and drinking baboon urine (it's true: look it up). Bonus: regale your partner with unsolicited facts about the benefits of eating the placenta.

Nine Months of Bliss

(One Woman's Infuriatingly Unrepresentative Experience of Pregnancy)

"Hi there, first-timers! I wanted to share my pregnancy journey with you because, you know, I think we're all pretty much in the same boat. You'll read in all the pregnancy books horror stories about all the stuff that can go wrong, but my experience was a more run-of-the-mill pregnancy that I'm sure is a better indication about what to expect.

So, let's chat about 'morning sickness'. Or rather, the absence of it. I mean, I hear people talk about feeling queasy, but honestly, I was more worried about overeating than anything else. Not sure what the fuss is about there.

Weight gain? Well, I put on a few kilos, which I heard is pretty standard. Though, to be honest, I was kinda looking forward to the whole 'eating for two' thing. But nope, I didn't really have any of those cravings you see in the movies. Walk in the park, frankly. If I had a dollar for everytime somebody said to me "Oh, you haven't even put on much weight!" I'd be 37 dollars richer.

Oh, the sleepless nights stuff? I basically turned into a sleep champion, logging in those eight hours without any issues. Until someone in my mother's group complained about it, I thought pregnancy was all about the extra naps!

Now, labour pains. Okay, maybe I'm just super lucky, but it was more like intense discomfort than actual pain. Like, I was definitely uncomfortable, but I never had a 'grabbing onto the bed rails in agony' moment. Maybe I have a high pain tolerance? Or maybe everyone else is just being a tad dramatic?

So, here I am, holding my little one (who is fast asleep) and wondering what all the fuss is about. My pregnancy was pretty much a walk in the park, and I'm assuming that's how it goes for everyone. I mean, why wouldn't it be, right? We're all on the same pregnancy wavelength, I'm sure. Sending you all the best vibes for your super easy pregnancies. Have fun -- I did!"

- Bethanny

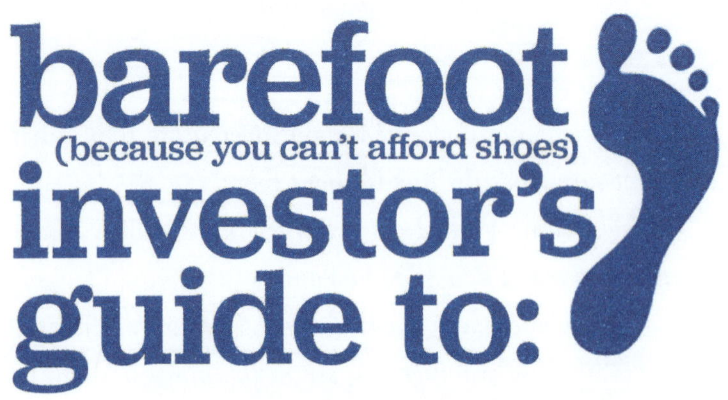

Pulling out the Welcome Mat

(from under your parent's feet)

Every parent, even the terrible ones, would like to put a safe and secure roof over their children's heads. However, with Australian house prices now slightly greater than the GDP of most Pacific nations, the idea of a dream home is now out of the reach of pretty much everyone except people who are lucky enough to have rich parents who died at an early-enough age.

If living next to a toxic waste site while dodging ice-dealer turf wars is not your cup of tea, luckily it does not have to be this way.

2023-24 will see double-digit growth in home prices. Per week. Rentals, meanwhile, will, of course, be worse. This means that pretty much every property in Australia is now slightly more expensive than Buckingham Palace. In a sample week in the second half of 2021, there were 83,142 capital city properties currently on the market. Of those, average income-earners were able to afford approximately 12. And 11 of those were car parking spots.

Perhaps you are lucky enough to own a small property. A cosy apartment where you can put a load of washing on, unstack the dishwasher and throw a frozen pizza in the oven, without ever having to move your feet. Of course, your children could be quite happy living in such close quarters. Walking is not really a thing amongst kids anyway nowadays, unless Nintendo releases a game that requires it.

You can stack their cots on the shelf space next to your desk in the living room. Hell, the built-in cupboard in the bedroom is basically another bedroom if you malnourish them enough so they don't grow very tall.

Of course, they would be happier in a sprawling four-bedroom federation house, with a leafy garden and room for a pool. The kind of house that your parents are currently enjoying, on their own, with not one shelf cot in sight.

Persuading your parents to spread their wings and fly the coop might require some longer-term strategic thinking. For example, you might deliberately rent a home in the catchment area for a school that keeps getting in trouble with various Royal Commissions.

When it comes time to enrol your child, you can point out to your parents the jail records of the gym teacher as a great reason for you to move to a home in a more desirable catchment area, such as the sprawling four-bedroom federation house, with a leafy garden (and even room for a pool) that your parents are currently enjoying, on their own, even though they don't have any school-aged children.

The Art of Loving Persuasion

You should not wait until you have children to begin the process of rearranging the deckchairs on your parent's sun-drenched deck. Many newlyweds are still picking the confetti out of their hair when they begin the process of 'loving persuasion' of their house-owning parents. It is important to look for the psychological flaws in your parents that you may have overlooked until now because you love them.

If you happen to have a father with a penchant for the pokies, a carefully orchestrated poker game can work

KNOW THE DIFFERENCE

Russula mushroom
(not deadly)

Death Cap
(deadly)

wonders on getting those titles deeds off him in a single night. A small investment in strategically placed mirrors, a remotely-located card counter and a wireless comms system can result in unimaginable returns.

Of course, sometimes parents have an unreasonably strong attachment to the house that they've lived in for the past 50 happy years. For them, simply wait for a particularly rainy summer, and then invite them around for "mushroom risotto" using locally-picked produce.

Say what you will about the judgemental, racist, sectarian bigotry of older folks. They trashed the planet and have overseen the largest increase in the gap of intergenerational wealth ever, but they sure knew how to buy a house and wait for its price to increase.

The Miracle of Pain

We asked a trained medical doctor, Dr Carl to give the missing picture in the process of labour: the male perspective. Here is his account.*

Whenever I attend a birth people ask me the same questions. Why is there so much screaming? Why the hell does this giant baby have to come out of this tiny hole? You're not my doctor, why are you even in this room?

And the answer to at least two of those questions is the same. It's because of evolution (or, if you live in Texas, God). When people evolved, for some reason the ones who survived were those who couldn't have children without screaming in agony for hours on end.

But the reason that childbirth is so stupidly painful is because of a phenomenon known as the obstetrical dilemma, which is a 'scientific hypothesis addressing the biological constraints imposed by two opposing evolutionary pressures in the development of the human pelvis.' Don't believe me? Well I copied that last sentence from Wikipedia, so take it up with them.

What does that mean? Well - and here I'm paraphrasing Wikipedia because otherwise I don't get paid for this

*Not to be confused with Dr Karl, which is why his wife made him throw out all his Hawaiian shirts

article (*you don't anyway* –***Ed***) - it means that when humans started walking it made sense for their pelvises to get smaller so they could run faster, but women also needed to have pelvises that can pump out a few kids. This explains why women used to be able to drop out a child and keep hunting but today need to give birth in a giant bath with music and a doula.

Still confused? Well on the left is a graphic I came across when looking for chimp porn, which may explain things more clearly. It compares the pelvis of a chimp, a woman called 'Lucy', who clearly asked to have her name changed when they photographed her pelvis, and a human. I think this graphic pretty much explains itself. At least I hope it does because I was performing in the Medicine Revue when we covered this in class.

Basically the obstetrical dilemma occurs because

Cervical effacement and dilation during labour

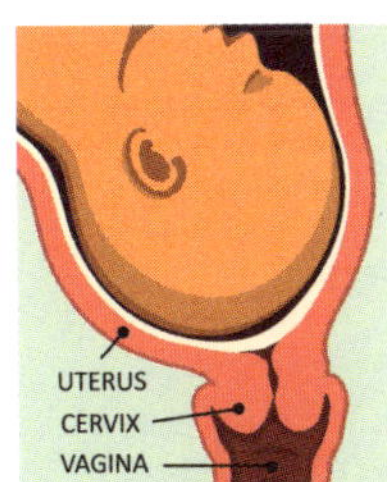

Cervix is not effaced or dilated

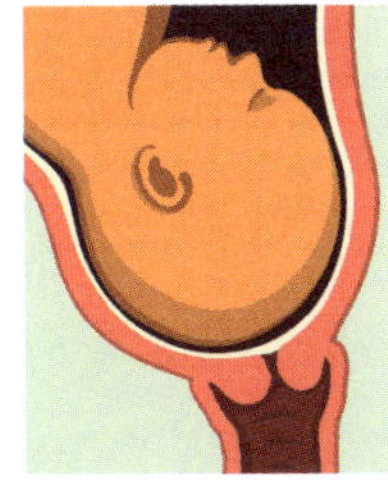

Cervix is 50% effaced and not dilated

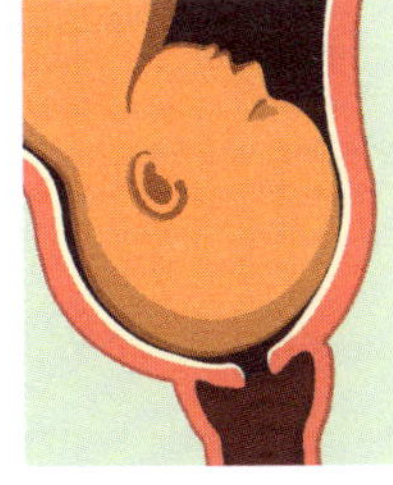

Cervix is 100% effaced and dilated to 3cm

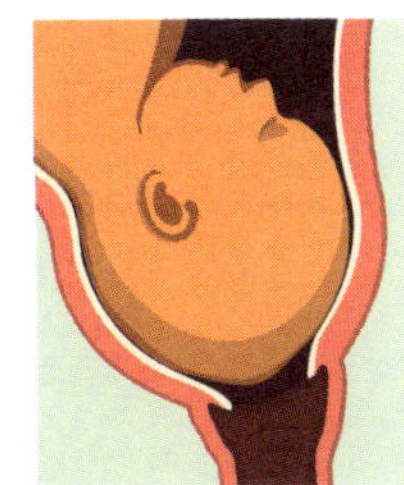

Cervix is fully dilated and what the fuck? That's not wide enough.

humans are so smart that our kids have big brainy heads but evolution makes us want to run faster so we can't just walk around with huge pelvises anymore. This is not to be confused with obstetrician dilemma, which is when your doctor refuses to charge you just the medicare prescribed fee and cracks onto your wife when you leave the room.

Caesarean section

One way to lessen the pain of delivery is Caesarean section, named, of course, after the famous birth of the Caesar salad. For convenience, this complex term is nicknamed 'C-section', which also happens to be my favourite seating area whenever I go to the football. Meanwhile, the operation itself could more accurately be described as a 'dis-section'. Of the mother.

Most doctors recommend a natural delivery rather than a C-section. This is because research shows long-term health benefits accrue, as you'd expect, to babies whose soft heads are forced through a narrow tube amidst a river of gore and filth. Despite this, C-section rates in Australia and the US are as high as one in three births. They're even higher in private hospitals, which is largely due to the better quality meals served during recovery. What an incentive — some of these palaces offer wine and cheese, for God's sake! Who wouldn't want their intestines lifted out and popped back in if it means a brief stint in paradise, eh?

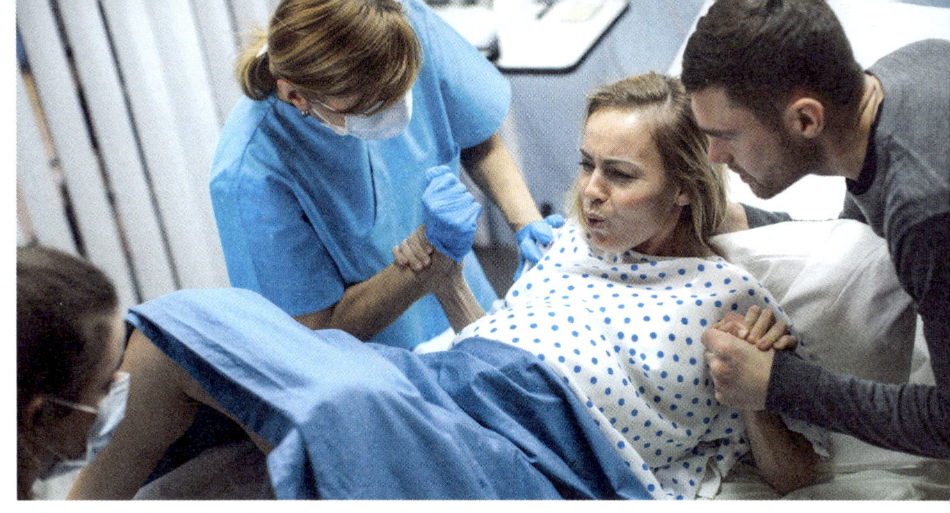

This is what it looks like when a person pretends to give birth

After labour

After the birth of a child I get a different set of questions from parents. Like, why won't my child ever sleep more than five minutes? Why can't babies look after themselves? And seriously you're not my doctor, how did you even get into my house?

And this, too, is mainly because of evolution. Unlike other animals, humans give birth to children well before they are able to look after themselves. Human babies are totally reliant on their parents and this lasts for the first 18 years of their life. 40 years in Sydney because they can't afford to move out.

This is because the human child is born with an underdeveloped brain. Scientists estimate that a human baby would have to gestate for 18 to 21 months to reach the cognitive level of a baby chimpanzee. Australian politicians

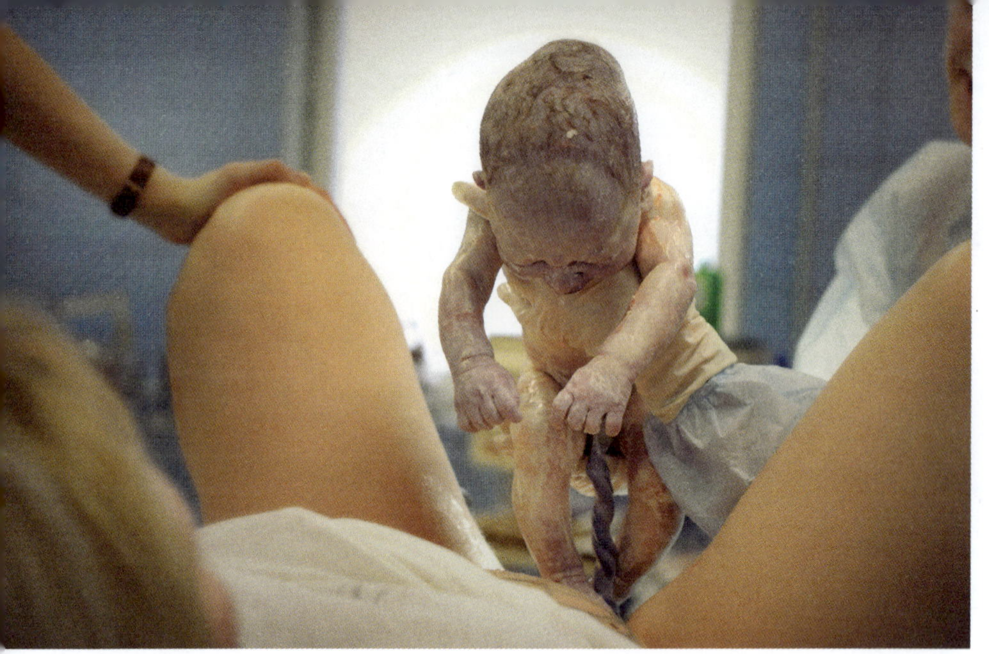

A slightly more realistic photo of what it's like

argued against this because it would make their system of paid parental leave seem even more inadequate. Children in Sweden gestate for 21 months. However, even there, it is controversial, with Swedish mothers saying there is no point carrying their baby for another whole year just so their child can talk to a chimp when he is born.

Scientists have suggested that the pain of childbirth could be avoided if humans evolved into a race with super wide hips and super small brains. It is still too early to comment, however, on whether the Kardashian experiment will be successful. So for the moment, parents are stuck with painful births and sleepless nights juggling a baby and smelling of spew. Thanks for nothing Charles fucking Darwin.

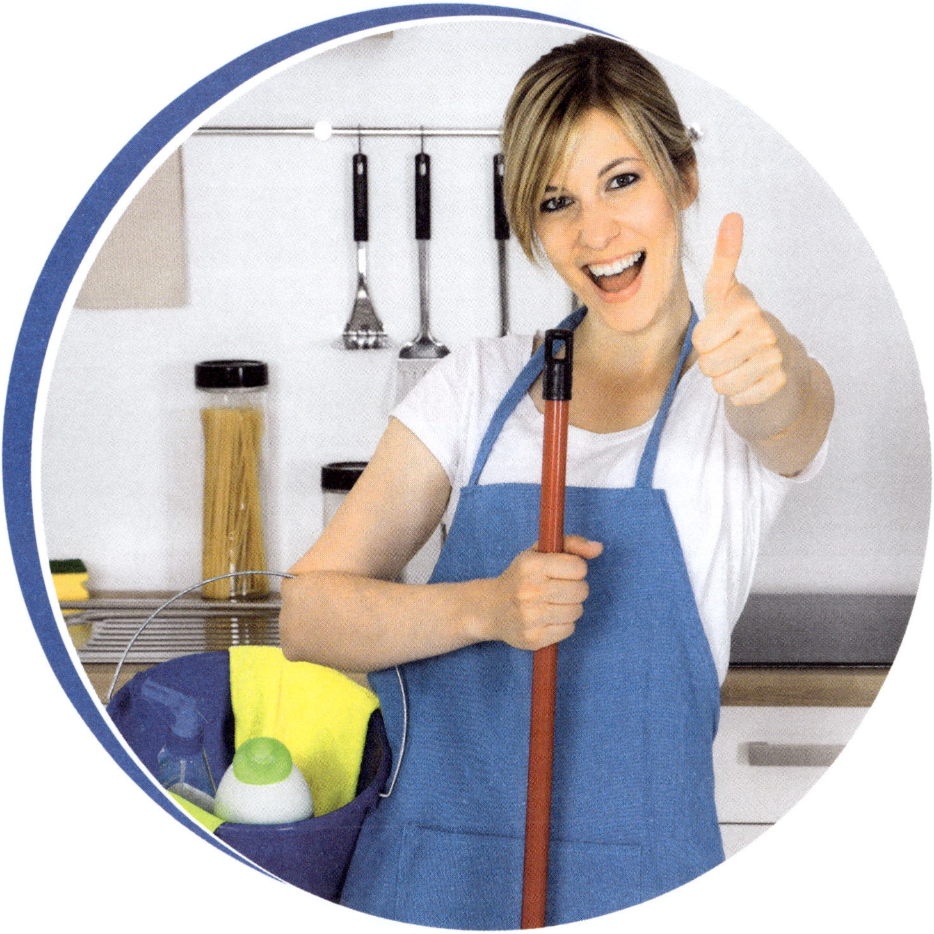

BUT HOW DOES SHE ENJOY CLEANING SO MUCH?

Wine and parenting is an art rather than an exact science. You want to balance flavours, weight and situation. A small fracas should be matched with a subtle wine and a full-blown tantrum with a sturdier wine.

THE TODDLER YEARS

Matching the Right Wine with your Disappointing Child

A special expert guide by Chris Taylor

Research shows that almost all parenting hurdles would be more efficiently resolved if only the parents in each case knew which wine to pair with their particular situation. So what should you be drinking with your next parenting crisis? I've nominated my Top Six Picks when it comes to matching the perfect drop with your imperfect child.

1. Your Child Is Bullying Other Kids At School

Parenting experts will argue over which Adelaide Hills chardonnay goes best with the shocking news that your child is a monster who frequently terrorises the other children in the playground, but I think the 2013 Shaw and Smith M3 Chardonnay will best capture the trauma of your discovery. The wine has light, subtle notes of oak barrel, melon and peach, which coincidentally are all things that your child has probably thrown at the heads of other children.

2. Your Toddler Won't Stop Crying

It's almost impossible to listen to the endless wailing of your newborn at night, without thinking of the Tim Adams 2010 Pinot Gris. There's a natural harmony between the wine's delicate, ripe fruit and the piercing screeches and caterwauling of your uncooperative infant. I'd suggest even giving a glass or two to the infant in question in a bid to shut him up.

3. Your Child Has Been Kidnapped

What better way to take in the news that your child has been abducted, quite possibly by an organised paedophile ring, than with a drop of the Hahndorf Hill Gruner Veltliner GRU 2014, which was recently described by James Halliday as "a perfect expression of post-kidnap anxiety." It's drinking very well now, but is sure to take on even greater depth and roundness in eight to ten years, when you finally start to accept that your child's not coming back.

4. Your Child Does A Massive Poo In Coles

It doesn't really matter what you drink with this particular situation – it won't do anything to improve it. My tip is to skull an entire bottle of tequila and hope that you pass out before the staff at the supermarket can identify you as the parent.

5. You Lose Your Child In A Custody Battle

For decades the acclaimed Eden Valley winemaker, Stephen Henschke, has devoted himself to the task of making a wine that perfectly expresses the character and delicacy of an ugly custody dispute. His Mount Edelstone 2012 Single Vineyard Shiraz came close, but not close enough for the perfectionist Henschke. Then, after years of perseverance and experimentation, Henschke finally had his eureka moment when he inadvertently sipped the dregs of his cellar door spittoon. At last! Here was a drop that reflected the true essence of a painful, protracted five-year battle in the Family Court of Australia.

6. Putting Your Child Up For Adoption

It must be one of the most difficult decisions for a parent to make. Whether the child is only a few days old or 32 years of age, the decision doesn't get any easier. However, a cheeky glass of Aziza Semillon 2015, from new-kid-on-the-block Harkham Wines, in the Hunter Valley, will pair beautifully with your heartbreak and distress. In fact I'd be surprised if you can stop at only one glass. As Robert Parker wrote in The Wine Advocate, "With such bright, zesty flavours and a vibrant citrus scent, it makes me wonder why I don't put my kids up for adoption more often."

INTRODUCING

HANSON'S

LAUNDRY LIQUID

The only way to make sure your whites and colours don't mix.

INSTANT REGRET

IT'S GOING TO BE LIKE THIS FOR THE REST OF MY FUCKING LIFE??

There are around about 1.5 million children aged between birth and four years of age in Australia. That is one-and-a-half million sweet little lives, filled with hopes and dreams and poo-filled nappies, and slightly fewer than thirty million sticky fingers.

In Australia, we have collectively decided to have our children later in life and are having fewer of them. Once upon a time, when a family had a dozen or more children, there was the artist, the dreamer, the scholar, the athlete, the clown and the one in prison who nobody talked about. Now, our one and only offspring is expected to fulfill all these roles, and more besides, as well as being the first-born and the last, and both the son and the daughter of the family. (Thank God for gender fluidity.)

Having one sibling does have its advantages, the main one being that you can crack hilarious jokes such as "You are my most moronic sister", or "You are my ugliest brother".

Family life is, however, a two-way street. Parents who have fewer children cannot afford to let any of them slip through their emotional fingers, so to speak. Parental attention is aimed squarely at their children, like a hot and uncomfortable closed circuit security camera run by a totalitarian regime that sees and remembers everything, or a modern social media platform. There are some good things, too, about being the child of an ever-present, ever-anxious parent who hovers just above their all-my-children-

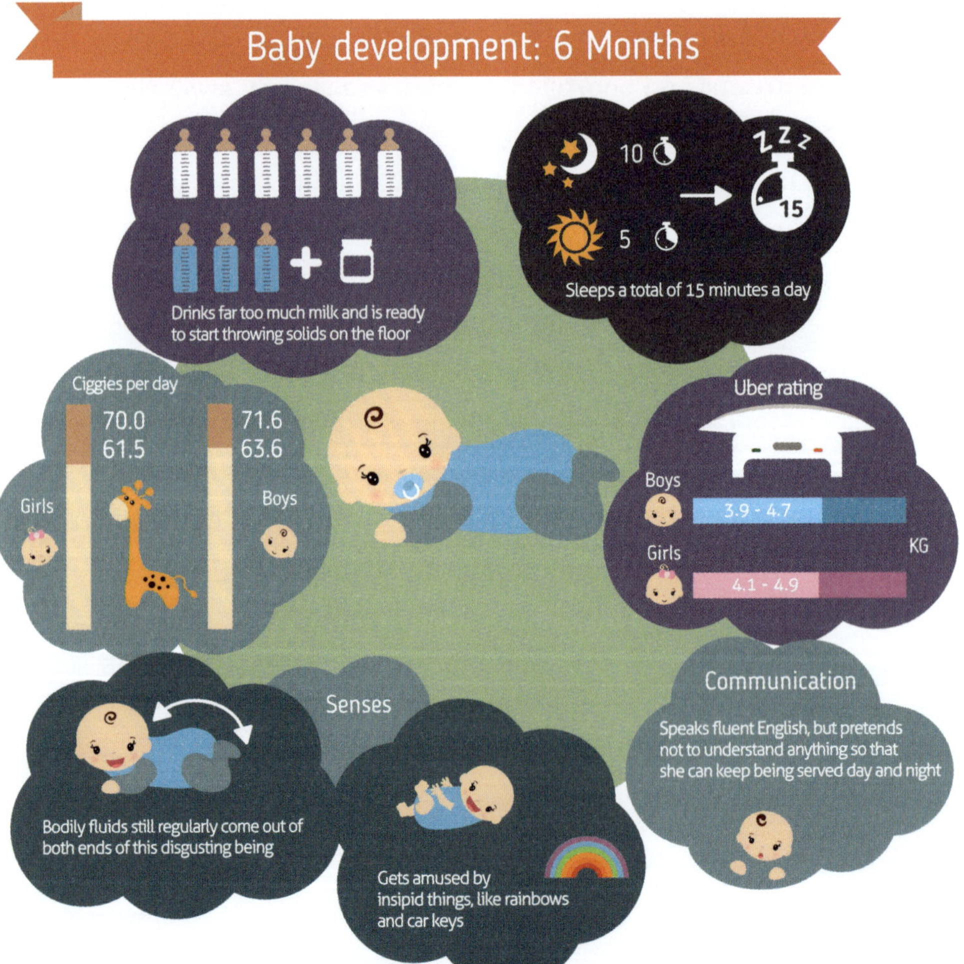

rolled-into-one child. These parents spend a lot of money on Christmas presents, they take Easter egg hunts and tooth fairy money very seriously, and they throw the most extravagant birthday parties in the neighbourhood.

Parenting young children is an exhilarating mixture of sleep deprivation, being tired, being fatigued, not getting enough sleep and being really exhausted. Sometimes, it's all of those things at once!

Many walking-dead parents can find themselves in a strange hallucinatory halo of complete indecision, half-decision making, poor decision making and then trying to remember what they were meant to be making a decision about in the first place. Young children, naturally, know that they can walk all over brain-dead parents, and so they routinely ensure that their parents remain as exhausted as humanly possible, while still being, technically, human.

For many working parents there is the exhaustion of child rearing, mixed with the weight of responsibility of holding down a job, while pretending that they are super-human and can do it all. When you realise that three-

quarters of your take-home pay is going directly to your children's daycare centre, you can start to wonder if keeping just one-quarter of your pay is enough to justify being away from your children for eight or more hours a day. It turns out it is. It definitely is.

We wanted to take a quick look at what we thought were some of the important things about life with a preschool-aged child. So, we have looked at children and parents buying, lying, partying, explaining, regretting, hoping, competing, winning and losing. Importantly we wanted to celebrate parents falling down and getting back up again. Perhaps it is true to say that getting back up again is what parenting is really all about. Enjoy!

The happiest this couple have been in weeks. It's a miracle the photographer got such an uplifting shot.

LYING IS GOOD

One of the wonderful lies that new parents tell is the lie about not lying to their children. Please do not burden yourself with the weight of guilt, as all parents lie that very same lie, (the one about not lying), over and over again, and they actually believe it to be true. Some highly experienced parents might say that a solid base of lies can actually build a firm foundation for children's future lives. We have met those parents. We are those parents.

Vladimir Lenin once said that a lie told often enough becomes the truth. And he should know. A lot of people lied to him. Anyway, all parents lie to their children. And if you say you do not lie, then you are lying. We all remember the outrageous lies from our own childhoods and yet we continue to lie to our own children. It is hard to deny the reality that you simply cannot beat walking down the well-trodden path of a family tradition. J.M. Coetzee summed it up so brilliantly, by saying that our lies reveal as much about us as our truths. And that is no lie. In the fullness of time your children will be grown up and you will be old, and your children will start confidently lying to you about the accreditation of your aged care residence. Karma, oh sweet and precious karma.

The lies we tell can range from the palest of white lies

that offer praise and encouragement to an insecure child who has no talent for finger-painting, to the dark and lingering deceptions that can last a lifetime and that will never be forgiven, nor forgotten. It is sometimes said that the seeds of doubt, once planted, will grow, but in the spirit of keeping it light, let us concentrate on those funny little 'embellishments of the truth' because they are the lies that hardly ever ruin children's entire lives. Well not very often, at least. Our anonymous committee of 'sharing parents' (otherwise known as 'sharents') has provided the following gems:

"We told our toddler that Father Christmas watches him all year long and monitors his vegetable intake. We called it the 'veggie register' and our son soon started referring to the 'veggie reggie' with great solemnity. Our son honestly believed that there was a direct correlation between eating up all his vegetables and getting Duplo for Christmas. Without this little lie our son would now be dead from a diet consisting solely of hot chips and burgers."

- Bettina, 32

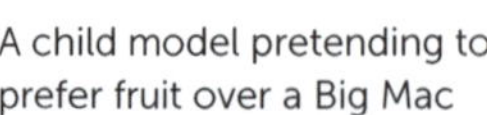

A child model pretending to prefer fruit over a Big Mac

A child model doing a pretty poor job of pretending to be asleep

"Our six-year-old lost his first tooth and he was so excited at the prospect of getting some money from the tooth fairy. That night we told him that he had to get off the iPad and settle down to sleep, as the tooth fairy was unable to visit us because the iPad would interfere with her Sat Nav. He immediately closed his tablet, and closed his eyes, so we think he must have believed us. We have used the Sat Nav excuse a few times now. I will be sad when he outgrows this lie."

- Sanjeev, 29

"One day it finally dawned on my three-year-old daughter that the chickens in the barn eventually become the chicken we cook and eat. In horror she announced that she was never eating chicken again. Soon after, I made chicken wraps and I told her that the lumpy bit in the wrap was a chicken-flavoured, chunky mayonnaise. I assured her that this type of mayo is not

A naturalistic pose of someone holding two chicken wraps

made from chicken. Chicken wraps are now her favourite food. We call them 'lumpy wraps'."

- Shannon, 37

"It was a bitterly cold and windy afternoon, and my children were nagging me to take them to the local park. I dramatically looked out of the window, as if I were carefully assessing the weather. I then told them that 'they' close the playground when it is really windy because 'they' do not want little children to blow away. When they asked who 'they' were, I told them it was the police. My children did not really believe me, but I stuck to my story."

- Huss, 43

An AI depiction of a girl in an illegally windy playground

An AI depiction of this touching scene. Note the writing on the packet of chips.

"Despite my best efforts my four-year-old caught me as I was sneaking a packet of potato chips into our shopping trolley. I suddenly found myself telling her that the chips were not intended for us to eat but that I was buying them for our dog. I provided an elaborate tale of how much Tom Tom loved chips and that this was a rare, but special doggy treat for him. My daughter believed me, and when we got home, I watched as she fed Tom Tom by hand, one chip at a time, until the whole packet was finished. I am sure I learned an important lesson that day about lying, I just do not know what it was."

"We know nothing about fish, but despite this, we were gifted a lovely new fish tank. Our son was so excited when we went to the pet shop and bought two fish – a big one and a little one. One morning, when my son was at school, we noticed that only the big fish was in the fish tank and we assumed that the big fish had eaten the little fish. We did not want our son to be upset so we went back to the pet shop and bought a

Not entirely convinced the AI nailed this one

similar little fish to replace the 'eaten' one. When our son came home from school, he was amazed to see the new fish, which we enthusiastically assured him was the same little fish that we had always owned. He then led us into the laundry where the original little fish was happily swimming in the laundry bucket.

Our son had transferred the little fish to its new home that morning because he was worried it might get eaten by the big fish. We then confidently announced that the big fish must have had a baby."

- Mike, 35

The AI nailed this one. Who needs humans anymore, huh?

"Just before Christmas last year I took my little daughter to Kmart to do some shopping. She excitedly ran along the aisles of the toy section, pointing out all the toys that she wanted Santa Claus to bring her. I noted her selection and that evening I ordered them online. The following week there was a knock on the door and a courier delivered a very large box from Kmart. I was just about to hide the box when a phone call in another room distracted me. When I returned, my daughter had found the box and was overwhelmed with the excitement of

discovering all her new toys. She was puzzled as to why Santa Claus had delivered her toys during the day and not waited until Christmas. I answered that because she was the very, very best little girl in Australia, Santa Claus had decided that she should have her toys early. My daughter did not question this explanation at all."

- Tania, 43

"We were in a rush to complete some paperwork that required a passport photograph of each of us. I did not have a passport-sized photograph of my new baby, so I simply used a photograph of my four-year-old daughter when she was a baby. The paperwork was completed, and I was lodging it when my daughter loudly piped up, telling the officer that we had used a photograph of her, not of her baby sister. I laughed nervously and gently scolded my daughter, reminding her that she shouldn't make up stories. My daughter looked at me in a way that I have never been looked at before."

The young girl at the passport office, moments before her mother is arrested on fraud charges.

- Lisa, 35

"Every year our son's ballet school puts on an end-of-year dance concert for all the children's families and friends to attend. For last year's performance, all the children wore animal masks as they danced to the music from 'Carnival of the Animals'. My husband was filming the performance, making sure that there were lots of closeups of our son. My husband even filmed our son as he left the dressing room, walked along the corridor to the stage, climbed the stage stairs and appeared from behind the curtains. There was not a moment of our son's performance that my husband did not film. When we got home later that evening, we showed our son the video and he pointed out that we had entirely filmed his friend Benjamin. It turns out that our son was the lion, not the cat. My husband immediately said that he filmed Benjamin because his mummies did not have a camera phone and he thought they might like to have a video of Benjamin's dance performance."

It doesn't make a huge amount of sense that the father would be in a crowd of children if he's filming a school concert (he'd be sitting with other parents, right?) but I still feel this is the right vibe. Well done, AI. I'm going to go and sack our art department. I'll be back shortly.

- Frier, 44

Because babysitters are expensive
Pfizer
XANAX
0,25 mg ALPRAZOLAM

CREEPING REALISATION

Primary School Age: The Best (Drug-Free) Days of Their Life

Primary school age is the sweet spot of parenting where your children blossom into mini adults, minus the ability to pay their own way on household bills.

As they head off to school to learn the crucial skills of simple addition, avoiding creepy teachers and mixing baking soda with vinegar, it's a time for parents to bask in the glory of their offspring's newfound independence. After all, you're finally getting a taste of life without nappies and midnight feedings! But hold on to your parenting handbooks, because you're about to get a creeping realisation that these seemingly idyllic years are not all they're cracked up to be.

Artistic Masterpieces and Macaroni Art: Almost from day one at primary school, you will find yourself being made to gaze upon the gallery of your child's 'masterpieces', and marvel at their avant-garde exploration of finger painting. Each colour-smeared canvas is a testament to their burgeoning inability to convert their creative vision into anything worth keeping beyond a few weeks on the fridge.

The happiest days of their life

Homework Triumphs and Tears: Witness the miracle of their daily homework routine—a heartwarming saga of pencils vanishing into thin air and maths problems that can't be that hard. The textbook must be wrong.

As you guide them through their assignments, be prepared to channel your inner educator by furtively looking up Wikipedia. In no time, you'll find yourself pretending that your explanation of Pythagoras's theorem makes any sense, while wondering why you can't remember who Edmund Barton was.

Social Skills and Playground Politics: More stressful than any 4am nappy-change is watching from afar as your precious offspring navigate the delicate social ecosystem of the schoolyard. From losing friendships over Pokémon card deals gone bad to orchestrating complex trades involving lunchbox snacks, your child is becoming a budding diplomat / day trader / ruthless sociopath. And don't forget playdates—where instead of just sitting watching the kids play in a sandpit, you're now expected to be an event planner, therapist, hostage negotiator and snack distributor all at once.

Cultural Phenomena and Parental Confusion: As they excitedly babble about the latest trends, be prepared to nod along while Googling terms like 'Fortnite' and 'Roblox', 'the ideal temperature of dinosaur eggs to make them hatch' under the table. Welcome to the world where memes are the new currency and you're constantly three TikToks behind. Just try not to 'dab' in solidarity, only to find out that trend died 'about one hundred years ago'.

So, embrace the primary school age with open arms and a supply of Prime energy drinks (for you). These truly are the 'best' (and most perplexing) years of your parenting journey. Get ready to embrace the chaos, the un-vacuumable quantities of glitter, and the endless questions about why the sky is blue. It's something to do with the scattering of the light-waves in the upper atmosphere, by the way.

Enjoy the evanescent period when they still enjoy learning all your moves. It won't last.

The Phone Call

The phone call is a rite of passage that every parent of a primary-aged child must face.

As your little one navigates the tumultuous seas of childhood, you can rest assured that a call from the school or another parent will serve as a rude awakening, shaking you from the blissful delusion that parenting was all finger paints and playdates.

The Unexpected Accidents: It starts innocently enough—a call from the school nurse or a fellow parent. "Hey, just wanted to let you know that Tamara fell off the jungle gym and might have broken her arm." Cue your heart leaping into your throat. The panicked call to the other parent. The realisation hits that parenting isn't all about bedtime stories about being a superhero; it's about being the first responder to your child's shattered illusions of invincibility. And the boringly-long wait in the ER while the nurses attend to more life-threatening injuries than the fractured thumb of a perfectly healthy seven-year old. Thank God you bought them that iPad.

The Bullying Revelation: And then, there's the call that can send even the most composed parent spiralling: "Your child was bitten by another kid at school today." It shatters your delusion that you'll be able to protect them from every sling and arrow. They're their own person now. All you can do is help this tiny helpless being navigate it themselves. Devastating. The worst. Although...

When the Accused Becomes the Accuser: But wait, there's more—because what's parenting without a good ol' plot twist? Brace yourself for the ultimate curveball: "Your child is being accused of bullying." The shock is palpable as you grapple with the realisation that your own flesh and blood might be causing harm to others. It's a moment of reckoning, forcing you to reflect on the values you've instilled and the lessons that need reinforcing. Suddenly, the serene family photos and

A future Liberal Party staffer chatting to his colleague about the importance of merit-based preselection of candidates.

"I'm sorry ma'am. I've got some bad news. Your son has been involved in a preselection and is now the leader of the Federal Liberal Party."

art projects feel like a distant memory in the face of this uncomfortable truth.

For many, 'The Phone Call' is the moment when parenting collides with the real world. It's a stark reminder that alongside the joy of raising a child, there lies the responsibility of guiding them through the messiness of life—a task that requires a strong stomach, an open heart, and, most crucially, the ability to not just be guided by how your own parents would have responded, but instead be guided by your own judgement and values, mixed with vast quantities of loving trust in your child, no matter how much of a shit they may have been.

The Shoe Industrial Complex

During the primary school years, kids' feet grow so fast that keeping up with the right shoe size becomes a full-time job. You may find you need to quit your day job so that you have enough time to keep up with your shoe-buying responsibilities during this period.

Kids' footwear is rendered obsolete at an astonishing pace. This dynamic engenders a relentless demand for larger sizes, prompting parents to engage in an ongoing cycle of shoe procurement. Economically speaking, this cycle exhibits characteristics reminiscent of a subscription-based model, where continuous engagement and expenditure are essential components.

It's like subscribing to Netflix, but it costs $200 a month and every show disappears before you've finished watching them.

The financial implications are striking. Amongst primary-school aged parents, 157% of income is spent on shoes, leading some economists with primary-school aged kids to propose cutting kids' feet off instead. It would certainly be cheaper.

Growth Spurts (and How to Stop Them)

Growth spurts are a huge bore and to be avoided at all costs. Not only do you need to pay for larger clothes, bigger bikes, scooters and even beds, you also have to stump up for vast quantities of food. Luckily, there are three ways to put a lid on your child's trajectory.

1. The Power of Shame: Picture this: your child asks for a second helping of roast chicken. You pick up the carving knife, and chirpily counter, "Okay, Lizzo."

Cue the dramatic gasp and the slow lowering of the fork. By subtly endorsing all the worst signals from modern culture at your dinner table, you can playfully plant the seed of doubt in those growth spurts, saving crucial dollars

GREAT DEALS

ON AFRICAN ORPHANS!

At Branjelico's, we aim to fill not just your hearts, but also your pockets. Our adoptive projects are selected shrewdly, for the canny modern adopter, who wants more than just love.

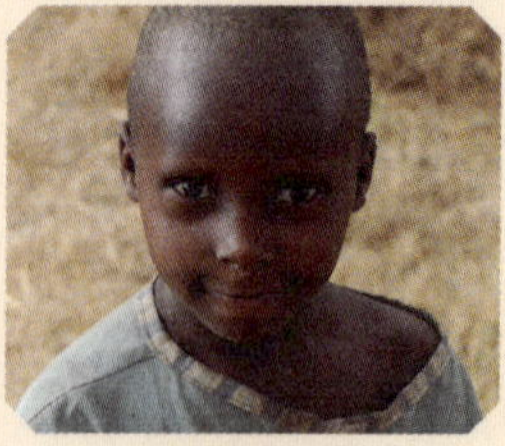

Kodwo, 4, Uganda - $48 000
Kodwo has been nourished by the good folk from Benedict Mission in Kampala. His androgenous bone structure and soft skin make him perfect for all kinds of modelling - from swimwear to haute couture.
Expected Return on Investment (ROI): **Six years**

Ndale, 7, Malawi - $1 million
Ndale is our finest ever acquisition. His exquisite lines and formidable poise mean he's ready for the catwalk today. Groomed by the priests from His Holiness's Home for Unattended Boys in Lilongwe, Ndale knows just how to keep his new parents happy. Ndale represents powerful financial value together with priceless intangibles. Don't miss out!
Expected ROI: **Five years**

Zakiya (5), Zalika (7), Zahra (3), Zubaidah (6) & Brian (4), Eritrea - $1200 for the lot
These siblings are healthy but HIV positive. Except for Zalika. She has AIDS. All can fetch water, grind barley & wheat, and can repeat some of the alphabet. Medication costs are $2300 per day but life expectancy is not great.
Expected ROI: **no**

Isoke, 6, Zimbabwe - $190 000
Snatched from Mugabe's militia at birth, Isoke has proven a natural for Kmart shoots. Already a nice little earner, we expect her photogenic traits to improve, not weaken, with time. Possessing an exuberance and joy known to westerners only through fictional characters, Isoke is likely to spark your own spiritual renaissance, or shit you to tears, only time will tell.
Expected ROI: **Three years**

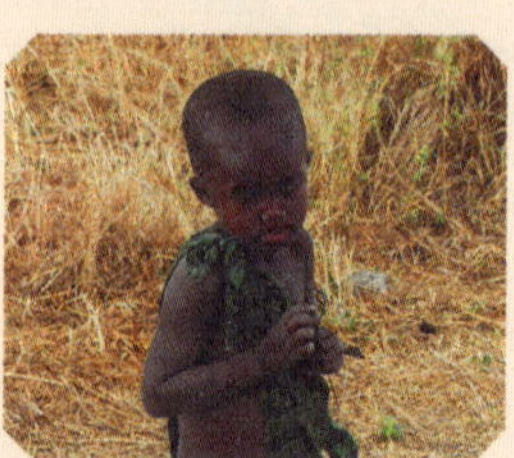

Umbandi, 3, Uganda - $50 (pickup only)
Umbandi comes to us through an agent known only as 'Joseph K'. Many more like him. Skills unknown. Full of potential.
Expected ROI: **n/a**

Sekele, 17 years, Kenya - $360 000
Sekele recently passed his A-levels, earning a place in the record books as the poorest person ever to ace the English end-of-school examinations. Living on less than $2 a day, Sekele has struggled to stay alive, but had no difficulty in earning a scholarship to Oxford to study quantum physics. We expect Sekele to return your investment within **Four years**.

at the grocery store.

2. Make Terrible Tasting Food: What if the food that usually gets devoured within seconds suddenly tasted, well, less than delicious? Instead of minced meat, use rolled oats. Suddenly your child's body will associate growth-spurts with terrible food. Mackeral and turmeric on rye bread for dinner, anyone?

3. Use Experimental Drugs: Imagine concocting a 'special' drink for your child. Now, we're not suggesting anything wild here, but perhaps a dash of the latest experimental growth-inhibiting drugs in their morning smoothie, might give them an extra year or two in their size 7 school uniform.

Terrible tasting food goes much further than delicious stuff

Strategic Peer Pressure: Crafting Your Child's Social Circle

Peer pressure is terrible. It is an enormously powerful force that can make your kid do things that completely go against their better judgement. However, it's a natural part of growing up, and since it's not going away any time soon, you might as well leverage it for your own benefit.

In particular, you can subtly harness peer pressure to sculpt your child's friendships into advantageous connections. After all, who said parenting wasn't an exercise in networking and living vicariously through your offspring?

The Strategic Friend Categories

1. The Professional Pipeline Pal: Pressure your kid into making friends with the loner goth whose parents are esteemed professionals. Not only will your child learn the art of self-interested schmoozing from an early age, but they might also open doors to invaluable connections for your own future endeavours. Your kid's friend's mum is a powerful barrister. Maybe you could get her to help you sue a former business partner? Remember, it's not about what your child wants; it's about your potential access to cocktail parties filled with decision-makers.

2. **The Convenient Co-Soccer Practitioner:** Get your kid to make friends with a soccer buddy whose parents live close to practice. You can strategically arrange for delightful post-practice beverages at their place. Your child's presence at their house also doubles as a reason to socialise, giving you ample time to build that contacts list.

3. **The Beach House BFF:** Encourage your child to befriend a kid whose parents own a nice big beach house. It isn't just for your child; it's an investment in your family's future summer getaways.

Teach your kids that having friends is all about location, location, location

Living Out Your Unfulfilled Dreams Through Your Child

Peer pressure isn't just about pressuring them to pick the right friends, it's also useful for projecting your unfulfilled desires onto them. Connect your child with the prodigy who reads books, plays tennis, and graces the school orchestra. Their influence will propel your child into pursuits that you always meant to embrace but never quite got around to.

Strategic peer pressure is a fine balancing act—crafting friendships that serve your immediate interests while giving your child an opportunity to live out your unfulfilled desires. In return, they will learn from you the invaluable lesson of how to do the same thing to their children. Remember, it's not manipulation, it's just strategic parenting!

KIDSPLAINING

Mansplaining is the act of a man explaining an idea or concept, usually to a woman, in a manner that is patronising and condescending. If a woman is not quite sure what constitutes mansplaining, they need only ask the nearest man to explain it to them. Many men will consider it their manly duty to do so, in expansive and mind-numbing detail. Mansplaining can be utterly infuriating and will certainly make your blood boil, but kidsplaining is worse, much worse, because you are not allowed to hit your children anymore. In essence, you should expect your children to display supreme confidence, backed up with very dubious knowledge.

We asked parents if they had ever been the victims of kidsplaining and we were not disappointed with their responses.

"My four-year-old told me, with a look of extraordinary confidence, that there is no gravity in our local library and that is the reason why all the books stay up on the shelves."

A local library which lacks sufficient quantities of gravity

Always wanted to be a tennis pro?
Make your kid become one instead!

A solar system on the roof

"My four-year-old borrowed a library book about the solar system. It just so happened that we had solar panels installed on our roof around this same time. He now tells everyone that he has the solar system on his roof."

"My niece carefully explained to her mother that the reason you are unable to see through closed doors and walls is because the black dots in your eyes (pupils) are getting in the way."

"My goddaughter loves to remind me that there are still lots of dinosaurs left on the earth, but they are hiding from all of us, because they do not want people to put them in the dinosaur museum."

"We were painting the walls of our apartment and our three-year-old demanded that we should paint the carpet too. She absolutely insisted that our floor covering was called 'carpaint'."

A dinosaur hides out of sight in a city, to avoid being put into a museum.

"I made my five-year-old granddaughter a quick dinner of fish fingers. She proceeded to patiently explain to me that this food was incorrectly named, as fish do not have fingers."

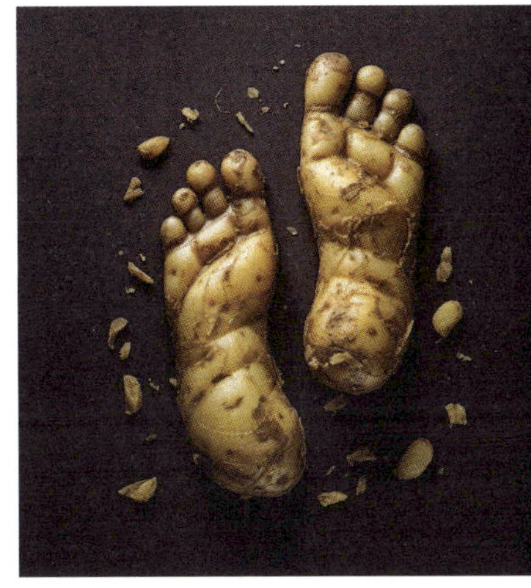

What toes are like before they stop being potatoes.

"My three-year-old step-daughter thinks that her toes were once potatoes and tomatoes and then, for extraordinarily complex reasons, the potatoes and tomatoes magically transformed into toes. We really want her to believe this forever."

"Our local shire council was giving away one free plant to every household. My daughter explained to the lady behind the counter that she was entitled to her own plant because she lived in her own house, on her own. My daughter is four."

"My six-year-old twins have always lived half of the time with me and half of the time with their father. When they were a little younger my children told everyone that the reason some fathers and mothers live together was that the daddy was probably too poor to have a house of his own."

Parenting a gifted child

*Is your child extraordinarily gifted? We asked Mamamia's Advice Editor, **Jane Frothington-Waites** to relate her experience of raising a gifted child, and provide tips to help you avoid the trap of soft expectations that so many parents fall into.*

Picture this. Your child is a straight-A student, head of the school orchestra, vice captain of debating, MVP in the state basketball team, and runs a charity program that supports orphans in India.

If that sounds all too familiar, then this chapter isn't for you. Seriously, vice captain? Cute, but I'd prefer not to get bogged down talking about mediocrity.

If your child truly is a high achiever though, read on as you could probably do with some advice. How best to channel all those talents? How to keep your child constantly stimulated? And when, exactly, to start the campaign push for SRC president.*

As a mother of a high-achieving child myself, I know how difficult it can be. I had to pull my daughter, Izzy, out of Little Athletics at the age of four because she wasn't being challenged enough. And in the 10 years since, while Izzy has cleared every hurdle put in front of her, society has continuously lowered the bar (or, as Little Athletics puts it, 'We need to give some of the other kids a go at the high jump.')

So I get it. It's hard being better than everyone else. By following these tips below, however, you'll ensure your child lives a rich, happy, fulfilling (but mainly rich) life.

Let them be themselves

Ah, kids. It's natural that they'll want to push the boundaries and carve out their own identity, especially as they grow older. What's important is you give them the freedom to be themselves, whether that's a straight-A student who plays state-grade tennis, or a straight-A student who plays state-grade netball. Or, in Izzy's case, a straight-A student who plays both.

Put aside your prejudices and just let them run their

*Kidding. If you haven't set up a campaign office yet, it's already too late.

own race - with you at the side cheering them on, while providing helpful tips for improvement.

Don't over-schedule

If your child is anything like mine, they'll be tempted to get involved in all of the many different activities at which they excel, leading to inevitable overload. So it's important that you teach your child to prioritise and make the right choices.

Just yesterday I had to counsel Izzy about whether to attend the dress rehearsal for the school's production of *Romeo and Juliet* (she's playing the lead), or the award ceremony for the Victorian Young Scientists extension program. In the end we decided she should be there to accept the award in person. I filled in as Juliet.

Spend quality time together

Don't forget to make time to just hang out together, without the pressures of school or extra-curricular activities.

Even something as simple as baking a cake together can be a relaxing, bonding experience. The different weights and measures required in baking also provide a wonderful opportunity to practice mental maths. I usually ask Izzy to make 1.17 times the required recipe, just for a little extension.

Make time for unstructured playtime

When your child has so many talents, it's tempting to pack their days with drama classes, choir rehearsals and overseas internships. To spark their creativity and imagination, however, children need unstructured play too.

For example, on Thursday nights between 7:00 and 7:30, Izzy has free reign to practice whichever instrument she wants. It's totally up to her which scales she chooses or which AMEB examination she wants to prepare for. We leave her totally alone, and make a strict rule of not interrupting or commenting on her unstructured play until we listen to the recordings afterwards.

It was only by having this total freedom that Izzy discovered the oboe (actually, she discovered the bassoon, but we talked her out of that – there's already a bassoonist in the Combined Independent Schools Orchestra). So she's found another passion, and I have another group of influential parents to get to know.

When cooking together, channelling a celebrity chef adds spark. I usually pretend I'm Gordon Ramsay.

Get involved in their interests

Becoming involved with your child's interests and hobbies is a great way to see the world from their eyes. Or in Izzy's case right now, from the eyes of Fyodor Dostoevsky.

For example, if your child is going through a Greek literature phase, as Izzy was in primary school, it's a chance for you to get involved in Sophocles and Homer too. If your child is going through a Pokémon phase, then it's a chance to get involved and shut that shit down as quickly as possible.

Beware of social media

Social media is a great way to let people know about your child's achievements. Snapchat and Instagram can be fun for kids, but it can sap their motivation and draw them away from their talents.

That's why I pay an agency to manage Izzy's social media accounts on her behalf. It means she can still maintain the largest social media followings among her friends, without missing out on rowing training or tap dancing.

Don't forget to maintain discipline

We all know the familiar refrain, "But I don't want to go to jazz ballet tonight!" Well, Mummy didn't want to make the two-hour trip out to Warrandyte on the weekend to watch you come second in the cross country championships either, but I did it, just for you. As the adult, you need to set rules as well as consequences for breaking them. I make Izzy stand in the corner until she's recited all the prime numbers in ascending order up to one million. But for your child it will probably be something simpler.

Love them

It's the simplest, yet most important rule of parenting. At the end of the day, all I want is for Izzy to be happy and to be a partner at a top-tier law firm.

Our family welcomes yours

Did you know that almost 93% of Catholic priests haven't yet been accused of paedophilia?

It's the perfect place for kids to learn and grow.

The Catholic Church

We touch people

Let's Get This Party Started

If you have a popular, socially competent, witty, engaging, happily well-adjusted child (apparently, they do exist), then your child will be invited to lots of children's birthday parties. If your child is none of the above, you will also find that they will be invited to lots of children's parties.

No matter how earnestly you encourage your child to become an introverted, socially-crippled sociopath, the invitations will keep on coming. Nobody knows why this is. It just is. Perhaps your life will be easier once you have accepted that your precious weekends will inevitably be spent driving your children to and from children's parties, irrespective of your child's personality type.

Some parents tell us that, in their experience, navigating the world of children's birthday parties is more complex and dangerous than *The Hunger Games*. So, as you venture forth into the world of fairy bread, musical chairs, helium balloons and staples-sticking-into-your-head party hats, may the odds be ever in your favour.

The first sign of an impending children's birthday party will most likely be the invitations. These can range from a deluxe, custom-made, gold-embossed, bespoke thermographic (that is where the printing is raised off the paper, we kid you not) textured scroll – all the way down the bottom to the hastily handwritten (and we are not talking calligraphy here) scrap-paper invitations, and everything in between. In some 'higher-achieving' parental circles, hard copy invitations have given way to electronic invitations, where the glitz and glamour remain undiminished. Recently we heard about an e-invitation that arrived in a parent's inbox in a personalised digital envelope, that showered confetti and played music when it was opened. The invitation contained links to Google maps, a birthday WhatsApp group specifically set up for the child's party, and RSVP tracking to ensure that you can run but you cannot hide. The invitation included a questionnaire from the venue asking about the invited child's possible food allergies and environmental sensitivities. The invitation also provided details of the birthday gift registry, which was comprised of a long list of presents that could be purchased for the birthday child, with prices ranging from $60 to $300. The kid was turning two.

Now that you have passed the party invitation test, the next hurdle to overcome is everything else. When you arrive at the party you might be asked to stay for a while to help your child to settle in. Do try to resist the temptation to go

If your child's party is not at this level of styling, then frankly, you've failed as a parent.

wandering off through the party host's house to make sure it doesn't have a Josef Fritzl-style dungeon. Remember, you are not there to judge other parents' lifestyle choices, but to drop off your child and get out of there as soon as possible. Remember, the sooner you can leave, the sooner you can start a no-holds-barred, wild and crazy party of your own, by which we mean, go home and clean the house until it is time to collect your (now quite vomitous) child.

All children's birthday parties can be divided into four distinct types.

The Arty Party

It is universally agreed that the Arty Party is as well-meaning, and yet, as ill-advised as any children's party could possibly be. Setting up arts and craft activities

The Arty Party: well-meaning, but ill-advised

might seem like a wholesome and creatively nutritious way to keep a dozen four-year-olds occupied but it's just not. There are always too many children, trying to do too much, all at once. Enthusiastic young artists gather as one, to express themselves through the visual arts. Painting, drawing, printmaking, stitchery, sculpture, collage, modelling, weaving - you get the idea. A large kitchen table, protected with only a thin layer of newspaper, is no match for the relentless application of "toxic-free" dyes, escaping watercolours, and glitter on everything. Fucking glitter. Suddenly you're asking yourself how the hell they got their hands on those Stanley knives, where did all the needles come from, and why are all the chopsticks being used as makeshift shivs?

The Literati Party

At first glance, this party seems harmless enough. Basically, all the children in attendance happily gather around and tell stories. This can be in the form of a **STORY IN THE ROUND**, where the children sit in a circle, with each child in turn contributing a line or two to the culminating story. There is the ever-popular **MIME STORY**, where a tale is told without ever uttering a word or the **RECORD TALE**, where the children record a shared story, complete with sound effects and music, and then share it with the group. There are puppet show stories, mock television news stories and rap stories for children from the 'hood. Older children enjoy bringing their tablets along and writing a chapter each of a collective story.

Instead, the quietest kid will derail the whole thing by almost immediately telling **GHOST STORIES**, which are far more violent than anything Stephen King ever dreamt up. The following are genuine ghost stories, told by a coven of five-year-old children. Once heard, never forgotten.

- The time the children got lost in the bush and were never seen again because a really bad kangaroo hid them in her pouch and never let them out
- One time there was an earthquake and a volcano and a tidal wave and an avalanche all at the same time and everyone at school got killed
- There was a baddie who had knife hands and gun feet and he walked along the street and everyone who passed by him got stabbed and shot until they were all dead

- There was so much blood because everyone accidentally cut their heads off with giant scissors that were hanging from the ceiling (this one was generally considered hilarious rather than scary)

If you want your kid to sleep ever again, skip this type of party. Luckily, Literati Parties are very rare nowadays, as nobody reads books anymore.

The Smarty Party

This is a party for all the fabulous children who think that they might not easily fit into the sometimes-stultifying parameters of a normal party. The Smarty Party is around and tell stories. This can be in the form of a **STORY IN THE ROUND**, where the children sit in a circle, with each child in turn contributing a line or two to the culminating story. There is the ever-popular **MIME STORY**, where a tale is told without ever uttering a word or the **RECORD TALE**, where the children record a shared story, complete with sound effects and music, and then share it with the group. There are puppet show stories, mock television news stories and rap stories for children from the 'hood. Older children enjoy bringing their tablets along and writing a chapter each of a collective story.

Instead, the quietest kid will derail the whole thing by almost immediately telling **GHOST STORIES**, which are far more violent than anything Stephen King ever dreamt up. The following are genuine ghost stories, told by a coven of five-year-old children. Once heard, never forgotten.

- The time the children got lost in the bush and were never seen again because a really bad kangaroo hid them in her pouch and never let them out
- One time there was an earthquake and a volcano and a tidal wave and an avalanche all at the same time and everyone at school got killed
- There was a baddie who had knife hands and gun feet and he walked along the street and everyone who passed by him got stabbed and shot until they were all dead

The Karate Party

It starts off so well. Bright-eyed and shiny-faced youngsters don their white karategis and solemnly bow to each other, while respectfully whispering 'onegaishimasu'. You have hired a responsible and well-meaning sensei, to carefully instruct the children in this ancient and refined martial art. Soon, however, the young grasshoppers' carefully regulated karate moves transform into choke holds, overhead slams, guillotine chops, axe kicks, and the notorious spinning back kick. Despite the sensei's best efforts, the karate party has transformed into a UFC cage fighting party. Even though it is an abomination of copyright law, not to mention, genre-confusion, most fights at this party will ultimately resort to a battle of Darth Vader-style Force grips. Bruises fade, but the memories never will. This is widely considered the best type of party, and should be tried at least once by every parent.

"To the barricades!"

Styles of Parenting

Every parent is too much of something. We cannot describe all of them so we have just chosen a few of our favourites. These ones. Feel free to add your own. But not here. This is our book. That would be too much.

The Think-Too-Much Parent

We have all been this parent, so welcome to our club. These are the parents who find themselves rolling and thrashing about on a wild sea of anxiety and alarm, while bravely trying to sail a boat made from good intentions. This is the parent who is certain that their baby will never learn to eat, drink, sit up, walk, talk, play, live, laugh … you get the idea. This is a club for parents who live in constant fear that their child will choke on water, who think that

"Kids! If you run around like that, you'll brain yourself on the coffee table!"

All At Sea

Think it might be easier to just dump the body at sea? Think again. In Australia, burials at sea are regulated under the Environment Protection (Sea Dumping) Act 1981. This means that you will need to apply for a sea dumping permit. This is where things can get a little tricky, as you are usually only permitted to be buried at sea if you can prove you have a strong connection to the sea, such as long-serving navy personnel or if you are a fisher. The body must then be prepared in accordance with the Ship Captain's Medical Guide, it cannot be embalmed, it must be sewn into a shroud (coffins are not permitted) and weighted sufficiently to ensure rapid sinking and permanent submersion of the body in a depth greater than 3000 metres. The burial must take place a long distance offshore, away from shipping lanes and trawling sites and the boat used to transport the body must be certified and equipped with GPS to ensure that the burial takes place at the precise and exact location designated. Are you still on board?

Fly Me To The Moon

If you have a spare US$2500 there is a company that will put your loved one's cremains into an Elon Musk SpaceX rocket and send these ashes into orbit around the Earth for two years. The company conveniently tries to gloss over the fact that, at the end of the two-year period, the rocket will re-enter the Earth's atmosphere, in a blaze of flames. The unapologetically designed for clever children, who have big, bursting, blossoming, bountiful, beautiful brains. Or brains that work a little differently from the usual kinds of brains. This is the kind of party a child might go to when they want to spend time with other children who have absolutely no inclination to find fault in the way other brains work. This is a party where nobody is on the spectrum because there is no spectrum here. This is a children's party where the C-words are freely used: crosswords and cards and computer coding and cosplay and classical musical chairs and charades and chess. This is the kind of party where the seeds of children's inner-braininess can flower into a blossoming tree of nerdy nirvana. And it is a place where nobody will criticise them for using the term 'nerdy nirvana'. Hop on the train to The Smarty party, where every child is celebrated and accepted, even the really, really annoying ones.

(Credit: Johnnyamoeba87/ Shutterstock)

a tiny knee scratch could develop into gangrene and who have decided that mortal danger lurks around every corner. Every table corner is a potential eye-blinder, every staircase is littered towards the top with the bodies of dead toddler sherpas, every playground contains at least one snotty-nosed Hannibal Lecter, ready to eat your child's liver with fava beans, washed down with a Cottee's Coola Cordial.

This is the club that welcomes members who are sometimes crippled by their own self-doubts, who are convinced of their own parenting failures and who wish that their intrusive thoughts of parental ineptitude would simply fade away. It would be easy to say that the answer is to simply care less about your child's health, happiness and well-being, but that advice looks a little bit dodgy when you see it written in print. Be brave our 'think-too-muchers'. We see you. We hear you. We are you. We will always be you. We have no idea how to help you.

The Pink-Too-Much Parent

The late, great Douglas Adams believed that a garden was beautiful enough without having to believe that there were fairies at the bottom of it. Well, dear Uncle Dougie, not according to the army of (mostly) little girls who believe, with all their precious hearts, that these fairies-in-residence are surreptitiously hiding in gardens, just managing to

"Kids! Dinner's ready!"

stay out of sight, but never out of mind. These children effortlessly believe in fairies and unicorns and mermaids and pixies and elves and pink. They really, truly believe in pink. And purple. But mostly pink. It is not so much a colour, but a way of life, and the pink-too-much parents have accepted (grudgingly or willingly, we cannot say) that their (mostly) daughters and (some) sons have opened their arms and embraced the world of pink. One of our pink-too-much parents told us a story about her twin daughters who believe that a day without pink is a day not worth living. They wear only pink, sleep in bedlinen of pink and play with toys that are overwhelmingly pink. The girls have now decided that they will eat only pink food, which is proving tricky because no child should eat a diet entirely consisting of watermelon, grapefruit, ham and rhubarb, and it tends to lead to a lot of only pink vomit. The parents have valiantly attempted to add pink food colouring to lots of things in the good food pyramid, with very mixed results. Let it be said, as we hoover up another mound of fairy dust, that life is too short to wage a colour war against a hue as beloved as pink, so our advice to exasperated pink-too-much parents is to 'think pink' and accept that too much pink is barely enough. Your (mostly) daughters and (some) sons will thank you for it.

The Drink-Too-Much Parent

Everyone knows that the most expensive part of being a parent is all the booze you have to drink. While this is most certainly true, it also reveals an underlying truth. We drank

A mother's group chatting about the struggles of parenting over a quiet mug of vodka.

before we were parents, we drink now that we are parents and once our children are grown and are making their own way in the world, I assume we will still be drinking. By that time, you can drink with your adult children and not because of them. In one survey of parents, they were asked to name the most essential thing they carry in their baby bag and apparently the most popular response was 'alcohol'. The question is, are parents drinking too much? What constitutes excessive parental drinking in Australia? One mother told us that her weekly mother's group get-togethers had gradually devolved into an 'it's-okay-to-drink-during-the-day' group, so long as everyone remained reasonably classy, by which she meant that nobody was noticeably slurring their words. The group had thought about dealing with the stresses of motherhood by trying yoga, meditation and relaxation tapes, but Aperol Spritz did the job much better.

The On-The-Brink-Too-Much Parent

Never before has a generation of parents so carefully recorded themselves accomplishing so little. Many parents, when on the brink of any moment, important or not, seem to instantly produce a phone. A record of that radiant moment is then made and shared with the world. But what about the other 23 hours and 57 minutes of the day?

A parent enjoying watching a video of her kid playing

No banshee-screeching, tantrum-throwing, poo-soaked spawns of Satan are ever going to make it onto a parent's carefully curated social media stream. You are not alone if you find yourself wondering where these angelic children are to be found. While these precious sunbeams might delight and enthral their on-the-brink parents, the appearance of perfect children might be setting an unrealistic and unvaultable bar that blocks the view and stands in the way of realistic parenting goals. Perhaps it is time to put down your phone and pick up your child. Even if they are a bit sticky. It will wash off.

The Never-Sleep-A-Wink-Too-Much Parent

Some parents, with nothing but love and good intentions, have found themselves in the never-ending downward spiral of excessive over-scheduling. Undoubtedly this style of parenting comes from a good place, however, this constant need to pack a day with endless activities until it is at bursting point, might yield results for children that might give you cause for alarm. Ludwig Mies van der Rohe first said 'less is more'. It might just be one of the most important parenting lessons we can learn - that our children will survive if we let them stare blankly into the middle distance, while achieving absolutely nothing for a period of time. Okay, so they cannot engage in distance-staring for ever, but more than a little bit of it will do them no lasting harm. In fact, it might just do them a power of good. If you are 'willing to be chilling' you might be giving your child an important lesson in the three Rs: rest, relaxation and rejuvenation. There's also reflection, recuperation, recreation, repose and respite, so it should really be the eight Rs, but covering our Rs should not be our main focus here. The minimalist parent movement suggests that editing our children's lives down to what is only absolutely essential, and no more, might allow children to expand their creativity and pursue their own self-determined interests. If you are largely responsible for your own happiness, you might just work a little harder in the pursuit of that happiness. Doing for our children might mean they are not doing for themselves, so they might never fully appreciate the joy of doing absolutely nothing.

How to Monetise Your Kids

There are many reasons to have a child: love, continuing family legacy, a walking, talking kidney replacement. But while most parents leave their kids to unprofitable pursuits such as going to school and having a childhood, more savvy parents cleverly turn their children into profit machines. We asked ***David Ferrier*** *to run us through the top ways to make money from your greatest treasure.*

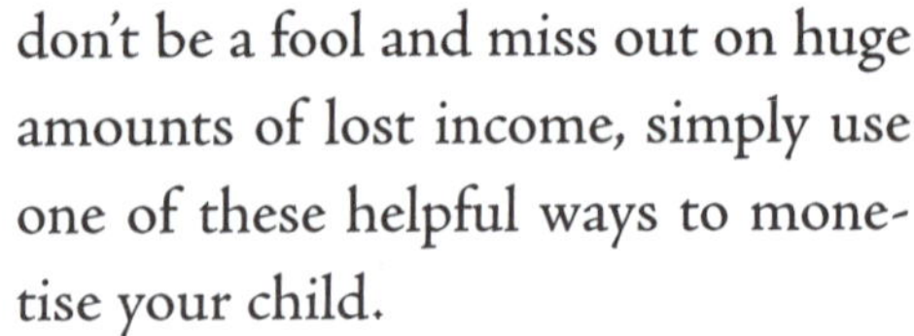

As Whitney Houston once said, "The children are our future," and they are; they are our financial future. So don't be a fool and miss out on huge amounts of lost income, simply use one of these helpful ways to monetise your child.

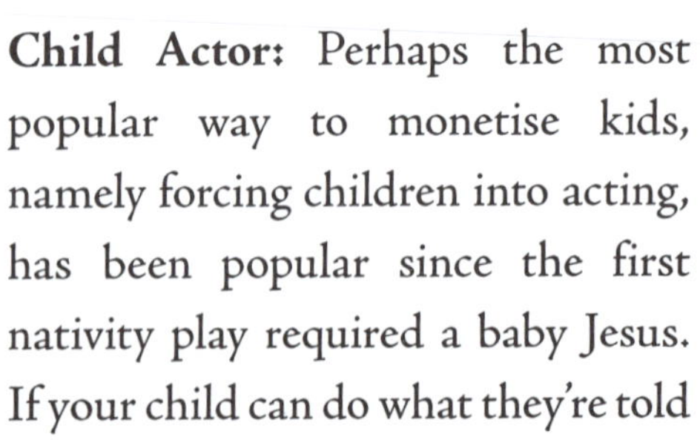

Child Actor: Perhaps the most popular way to monetise kids, namely forcing children into acting, has been popular since the first nativity play required a baby Jesus. If your child can do what they're told

Child star Macaulay Culkin at the peak of his ROI (return on investment)

and speak a few words while looking cute, child acting may be for you. It's also one of the few pursuits you can force your child into almost immediately following the birth. Once your newborn has plopped out of the birthing canal and you've decided on a name, a stage name, and a decent agent, before you know it, your child could be starring in the next instalment of the Baby Geniuses franchise.

Singing and Dancing: Luckily for parents, singing and dancing is one of the pursuits your child may actually want to do. If this is the case, grab a camera, film them singing, and upload it to YouTube. Soon your child could be the next Justin Bieber, touring the world and telling fans they make him sick. Even if your child is hilariously terrible, they will probably score you an all-expenses paid trip to Los Angeles to appear on Jimmy Fallon. It is worth noting that sometimes young singers and dancers don't become profitable until they're old enough to be marketed as someone an audience would want to fuck. As an added bonus, child singers and dancers often also make for great child actors! Diversify your income streams!

Beauty Pageants: Have you ever looked at your little girl and thought, "I think adults would find her hot!" If the answer is "yes," or, "yes, but only with a lot of makeup and

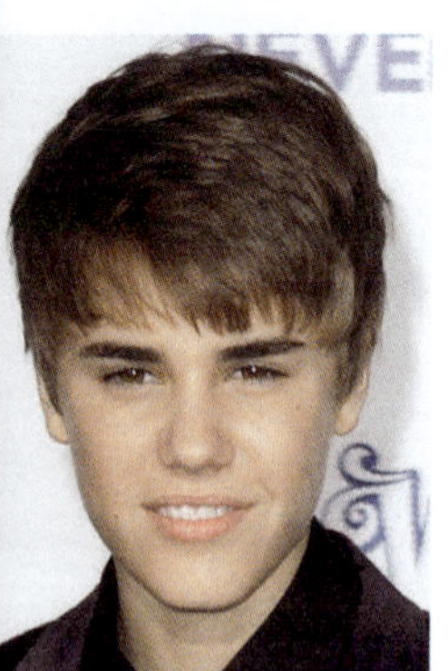
Justin Bieber once told Billboard magazine being a child star was "the toughest thing in the world". And to think people starving to death in the Horn of Africa thought they had it bad!

maybe a few sessions on a child-sized tanning bed" then maybe beauty pageants are for you. An advantage child beauty pageants have over other forms of monetisation is you will see the results of your investment quickly. It only takes one pageant to know if your child is a winner and therefore profitable. Conversely, you will know equally as quickly if she is an ugly loser. If this is the case, simply scream in her face about how much she has let you down, before going home and planning an alternative way to monetise.

Blogging: Did your child wet the bed? Did they throw a tantrum in the middle of the supermarket? Did they ruin your relationship with your partner, leaving you 'dead below the waist?' Well don't keep that stuff to yourself. Tell everyone about it on the internet! That's right, become a blogger! Blogging about parenthood, often known as 'mummy blogging', is an exciting new addition to the world of monetising children, kind of like how ISIS is an exciting, new addition to the world of global terrorism. It does not require them to have talent, looks, or privacy, they just have to be the disgusting creatures they naturally are. The beauty of parent blogging is that you're technically not forcing your child to work, you're simply exploiting their childhood and privacy to make tonnes of cash! Win win!

But how do you get started? It's easy. Next time your child falls over or shits themselves, don't immediately go to their aid; take a quick photo and write a Facebook post about how hard your life is and before you know it, sponsorships, paid posts and book deals will be flooding in!

True story: at the age of 13, Scotty Schwartz starred opposite Richard Pryor in The Toy (1982). Scotty then went on to star in several hard-core porn films!

Reality Television: Combining the strengths of many other forms of monetisation, reality television is the Frankenstein's monster of profiting from your children. If your child sings, dances, acts, competes in beauty pageants, cooks, cries, or believes they can speak to the dead (*Psychic Kids: Children of the Paranormal*) reality television is a way to make money simply by letting a film crew capture your everyday life. Some people even get reality shows simply by having a lot of children! (*Kate Plus 8, 19 Kids and Counting*). No talent required and think of all that fun sex!

IMPORTANT NOTE: If pursuing reality television, ensure your children have not molested anyone (see: Josh Duggar)

Will They Ever Move Out?

Navigating Your Child's 20s and 30s

The journey of parenthood used to involve watching your little ones grow, flourish, and eventually spread their wings to venture out into the world.

Nowadays, the prospect of your adult children finally moving out is about as likely as finding a unicorn riding a rainbow on a room-temperature super-conductor.

They Can't Afford to Move Out But That Doesn't Mean It's Not Their Fault

The vast overreach of capitalist accumulation and soaring property prices have joined forces to create the perfect storm of stay-at-home millennials and Gen Zers. You're not imagining it; this is a very real phenomenon.

But even though external forces are to blame, it's essential to direct your frustrations toward them instead. You must always remember that despite the economic hurdles they face, your child's inability to move out is their own fault, even though it's not.

This is crucial. By blaming them you can absolve

yourself of any nagging pangs of guilt your generation has about the bigger picture which caused this clusterfuck.

Navigating Their Long-Term Stay

So, how to deal with adult kids at home? Here are some handy ideas:

- Convince a local production company to turn your situation into a reality show; they'll either move out to escape the cameras or become overnight sensations.
- Enforce mandatory bedtime stories, reversing the roles, where they read the tales and you get tucked in.
- Insist that they spend at least one day a week helping you operate your Apple TV.

But probably the best way to get rid of your adult kids is to feign a back injury that requires them to bring you all your meals in bed. Even if they don't move out, at least you've now got a 24-hour butler. It's a true win-win!

Two models pretending that adult kids enjoy spending time explaining how to operate simple-to-use technology to old people

The Resentment Years

It is difficult to think of something that is so lovable and yet so frustrating as an elderly person, except perhaps for tequila.

Anyway, old folks can be funny and charming and sweet and wise, and they can also be none of those things. And therein lies the dilemma. Just how much care and protection should we provide for the elderly members of our family? How much of our care and protection do they actually need or want? Should we let them try and then fail and then learn from their experiences, or should we simply take the view that if they have not learned anything useful in the past 85 years, it is probably too late by now.

In some cultures, the elders of the group are honoured and revered. In other cultures, older people are seen as doddery old denture-wearing, walking cane-using nuisances who use imperial measurements, who talk about 'the old money', who wear floral aprons and who think colonialism has been given a bad rap, by the natives. Also, they call first nations people, everywhere in the world, natives. Also, some old blokes wear bandannas and that separates them from their fellow man in ways that cannot be easily overlooked.

Like most first world countries, Australia's population is ageing due to the sustained levels of low fertility (too much hesitating, not enough copulating) and the increased life expectancy (too much partying, not enough parting this world). This has meant that we have fewer children in Australia, and we have a much larger proportion of people who are aged 65 years and older. In other words, you might be the only adult child left in your family who can look after Grandpa and his ever-expanding collection of bandannas.

It is not all gloom and doom, however, as there is also a lot to enjoy in the company of older folks. Depending on their age, mobility, and willingness, you might be able to lovingly persuade them to be car space sitters, concert ticket queue sitters, house sitters, pet sitters, waiting-for-

In some cultures, older people are revered for their widsom. In our culture, they're revered for their free babysitting abilities.

the-parcel-to-be-delivered sitters and, of course, their true purpose in life, free babysitters. When you see the hourly rate charged by many babysitters, suddenly Grandma and her collection of teapots in the shapes of gumboots does not seem quite so annoying anymore. So, see if you can shake off the resentment that comes with knowing that your grandparents enjoyed a completely free university education and paid $6.20 for their house that has a double garage that is bigger than your entire, rented apartment.

The Art of The Dump

The number of Australians aged 70 years and older is expected to increase in 2024 to roughly 3.2 million people. That is a lot of cocoa, slippers and hot water bottles. Also, leaving voice mails. Seriously, just send a text.

For parents of young children, it can sometimes be an unsettling thought, that while you are busy parenting your youngsters, you are being parented by your parents. In close-generation families, your parents might even find themselves being parented by their parents too. This means that in some inordinately lucky families, a young child can be simultaneously parented, grandparented and great grandparented. What a privilege.

You might love the idea of your children having a strong

and enduring bond with their grandparents, right up until you realise that this means that you will also be spending more time with your parents. This should be avoided wherever possible. There are many ways to continue to distance yourself from your parents, while pretending that you want your children to get to know them. It's called the grandparent dump.

The Lump Dump

This is where you lump together a set of 'celebrations' and take yourself and your children to visit their grandparents just once, during that period of time. Simply lump together Australia Day, St Valentine's Day, St Patrick's Day, Easter, ANZAC Day and Mother's Day. Then there's only one left: the Father's Day, Halloween, Melbourne Cup, Christmas, New Year combo. If grandparents object to this style of dump, one mention of putting them in an old folk's home will keep them quiet.

The Bump Dump

You dump your children at their grandparent's house for the weekend, to enable you to bump your children's needs down your priority list, in favour of music festivals, sporting events, all-night dance parties, swinging or illicit affairs. Or best of all, sleeping in.

More experienced parents tell the grandparents that they will be working all weekend. If grandparents object to this style of dump, one mention of putting them in an old folk's home will keep them quiet.

The Ski Jump Dump

Young children do not belong in any ski resort anywhere throughout Australia. Kids are good at skiing but they will cramp your flaming Sambuca-fuelled, apres-ski hijinks.

Okay, so you might need to tell your parents that you will be working all weekend, however there is no need to mention that it will be your downhill slalom that you will actually be working on. If grandparents object to this style of dump, one mention of putting them in an old folk's home will keep them quiet.

HOME AND AWAY (FROM ME)

We're all busy, but even so, we all know that we should really make time to look after the ageing members of our families, and not just for the inheritance.

If you are finding that Grandma is taking up too much of your valuable time, keep in mind that it is not how much you are doing, but how much love you put into the doing.

The Australian Government operates the Commonwealth Home Support Program as well as the Home Care Packages Scheme, designed for people with greater or more complex needs. In an aged care budget of more than $20 billion, there are still long waiting lists for home care for older Australians. While there are more than 100,000 people receiving home care packages services, there are many more who miss out and end up passing away before they are provided with home care. This unfeasibly long waiting list has led many families to arrange and finance their own home care services for their ageing family members.

If Grandma is not too keen on having complete strangers lending her a hand at home, here are some ways you might be able to gradually convince Grandma that she really does need home care, provided by people who are not you.

Slowly Going Bad

Every time you call in to visit Grandma remember to talk about the increasing crime rates in her now-sociopathic neighbourhood. Together you can reminisce over the days when law-abiding citizens created a calm and reassuring place for everyone to live together in harmony. Now, of course, such days are gone, replaced with ever-increasing crimes and misdemeanours. You can pretend to read out these alarming statistics from the local newspaper on your tablet, even though it has not been in print for more than a decade. Grandma does not need to know that. Grandma does not need to know anything you do not want her to know.

In blood-chilling detail, you can invent details of street crime, aggravated assaults, bank robberies, arson, kidnappings, vandalism and even bloody mass murders. Of course, Australia's crime rate remains reassuringly low and steady, by world standards – but do not tell Grandma that inconvenient truth. Instead, you can carefully remind Grandma that a kindly home carer (who is not you) could protect her from the inevitability of a brutal home invasion.

Slowly Going Mad

Next time you are visiting Grandma and she wanders off into the kitchen to butter the kettle and put the scones on to boil, you can quickly rearrange the furniture in her loungeroom. It is a good idea to stealthily change things, hide things, turn things the wrong way around and generally make subtle, but observable changes to her home.

Not enough to entirely freak her out, but just enough to confuse and perplex her.

'I could have sworn I put my memory medication in this empty drawer'

It will do nobody any harm by talking, in grisly detail, about the life-threatening dangers of mossy pathways and slippery bathtubs. You might ponder out loud who would be on hand to assist Grandma if she fell and snapped her femur. Forgetful bewilderment is a good starting point in persuading Grandma that a home carer (who is not you) will be her passport to fully independent living. That is, living independently from you.

Slowly Going Sad

As gently as you can, you might like to remind Grandma that almost all of her life-long friends have died, or they have one orthotic-shoed foot in the grave. The fun and frivolity, the laughing until you cry, the rowdy revelry – all the joys of friendship will soon be nothing more than a bittersweet memory to her. Without unduly alarming her, you can let Grandma know that soon she will be utterly abandoned and alone in the world, without a familiar face or gentle hand to guide her through life's many travails.

When your grieving Grandma is mournfully staring into the abyss of imminent friendlessness you can cheerfully remind her that the family is more than willing to pay a home carer (who is not you) incredibly good money to be her new best friend, at least until the 'happily ever after' part of her life story.

GOLDEN SHOWERS

(And when we say that, we mean you will need to be showered in gold to afford to live in an Australian aged care home)

Ah, the golden years. So named, because our golden oldies will need to have accumulated their body weight in gold to pay for their aged care accommodation costs.

The Australian Aged Care Royal Commission has provided some useful data for examining the experiences of older Australians in residential aged care services. Currently, the average length of stay in a permanent residential aged care facility is almost 30 months. That two-and-a-half-years can represent wildly differing experiences for the residents, ranging from the bad and the mad to the pitifully sad. It should also be noted that some older Australians are glad they have found a warm and welcoming aged care home and consider their residency there to be an overall positive experience for them.

Some families are absolutely adamant that they will never put their beloved grandparent into an aged care facility, that is right up until the moment that Grandpa starts weeing into the saucepans and wandering down the street in his underwear in the dead of night. All of a sudden you can see some riveting pivoting going on, as adult children quickly realise that caring for a behaviourally-challenging older parent is not for the faint-hearted. And almost everyone turns out to be faint-hearted, when they realise that their saucepans are being totally ruined.

Now while the children and grandchildren might be immensely relieved that their beloved is planning to wander off to The Next-Step-Is-Heaven Nursing Home, they might not have realised that they would be asked to make a financial contribution to getting this antique roadshow off the road. Some families have ruefully described the payment process for aged care as a mean-spirited, means-tested outrage, where they have no choice but to sell the family home. To avoid selling up, some families try to pull the crochet wool over Grandma's eyes, by promising money that never eventuates. Rather than keeping Grandma in the glaucoma-induced dark, families should be upfront about not helping with the upfront costs, so Grandma knows where she stands. Unless Grandma is planning to use her secret stash of Bitcoins or Grandad is confident about his investment in the Nigerian royal family, many older Australians will have absolutely no choice but to finance their own admission to The Shuffle-Off-This-Mortal-Coil Nursing Home by selling the family home, to finance their residential aged care journey.

There is no doubt that the sale of the family home can cause great stress and anxiety to adult children, whose inheritance is now residing in a trust account at The Baby-Boomers-Get-The-Last-Laugh Nursing Home. It is what it is. So, Grandma, wrap yourself up tight in your suit of karma armour and relax in your luxurious, fully-appointed, independent-living apartment suite at The You-Get-What-You-Pay-For Nursing Home. You might just have had the last laugh.

An elderly couple delighted to find out how ruinously expensive the Australian property market is for young people trying to buy a home.

Death

The good thing about funeral arranging, is that there is a funeral to suit almost everyone's religious and cultural preferences, location, taste and budget. If you're lucky enough to die without a dollar to your name, the Australian government cheerfully pays for your final farewell, in what is optimistically described as a 'very basic funeral' service. They do not go into too much detail, so we are assuming there is no post-funeral drunken pub crawl that is sponsored by the government. Bloody typical.

While the funeral director will help you in many of the decisions involved in organising a funeral, we get the feeling that some of them probably work on commission, considering how strongly they try to sell you their most expensive funeral packages. Just be aware of the casket racket, as a cheaper coffin does exactly the same job as a more expensive one. Caskets cost from $2000 to $44,000. We are not exactly sure what $44,000 gets you, but we are hoping it comes with a free set of Airpods that your bereaved get to keep after the funeral is over.

The Guilt-Edged Funeral

Funerals cost $4000 to $20,000, but much higher costs can be incurred if you choose the 'guilt-edged' option. If you gave Grandpa a hard time in life then burying him in a diamond crypt is not going to assuage your guilt. Only alcohol can do that.

Crime Does Pay

In 2010, Carl Williams, drug manufacturer and ruthless gangland murderer, was buried in a bronze and 14-carat gold coffin that cost $30,000. Carl's grieving family (the ones who were not dead or in prison) scattered white roses and holy water, released white doves and balloons and travelled to the church, with their security guards, in a black stretch hummer. Carl, off course, was transported in a Mercedes hearse to his final resting place, with Tina Turner's *Simply the Best* accompanying the proceedings. Proceeds of crime have never been better spent.

Scatter Matters

Cremation is often seen as an easier and cheaper option than burial, not knowing that the storage and the scattering of 'cremains' can be both a can of worms (and ashes). To scatter the ashes, you'll need to get permission from the landowner if you're scattering on private property and from your local council or shire if the land is public. Scattering in some locations may contravene the provisions of the Protection of the Environment Operations Act 1997. You also need to ensure that you do not scatter on a windy day, as ash can be ridiculously hard to wash out of your clothes.

Death

The good thing about funeral arranging, is that there is a funeral to suit almost everyone's religious and cultural preferences, location, taste and budget. If you're lucky enough to die without a dollar to your name, the Australian government cheerfully pays for your final farewell, in what is optimistically described as a 'very basic funeral' service. They do not go into too much detail, so we are assuming there is no post-funeral drunken pub crawl that is sponsored by the government. Bloody typical.

While the funeral director will help you in many of the decisions involved in organising a funeral, we get the feeling that some of them probably work on commission, considering how strongly they try to sell you their most expensive funeral packages. Just be aware of the casket racket, as a cheaper coffin does exactly the same job as a more expensive one. Caskets cost from $2000 to $44,000. We are not exactly sure what $44,000 gets you, but we are hoping it comes with a free set of Airpods that your bereaved get to keep after the funeral is over.

The Guilt-Edged Funeral

Funerals cost $4000 to $20,000, but much higher costs can be incurred if you choose the 'guilt-edged' option. If company valiantly attempts to ease the unsettling horror of it all by saying that "... in a last poetic moment ... (your loved one will be) blazing as a shooting star."

The Cold Wars

Cryonics is the 'science' of freezing a recently deceased human being, with the intention of thawing them out and bringing them back to life. Some people believe cryonics is as simple as dropping the body in an enormous vat of liquid nitrogen. In truth, this would result in most of the cells in your body shattering. In fact, the process involves using a cryoprotectant (like the antifreeze used in your car) to slow down the formation of ice crystals in your organs and body tissue. Vitrification is what allows your cells to survive in a kind of suspended animation.

It can cost more than $200,000 to have your whole body preserved and around $60,000 to have just your head put in a Ziploc bag and tucked away at the back of the freezer. This heads-only process is called neurosuspension and relies on a whole lot more future technology being invented, in the future, for this to ever work out for you, in the future.

On a final, sobering note, it should be mentioned that no corpse has yet undergone this procedure and been reanimated. Also, at these prices, perhaps only rich, self-obsessed people are doing this, and they are not the kind of people you'd want to wake up and be surrounded by anyway. For God's sake, let your loved ones rest in peace in a warm, warm grave.